W9-ASF-013

3 1865 00272 3517

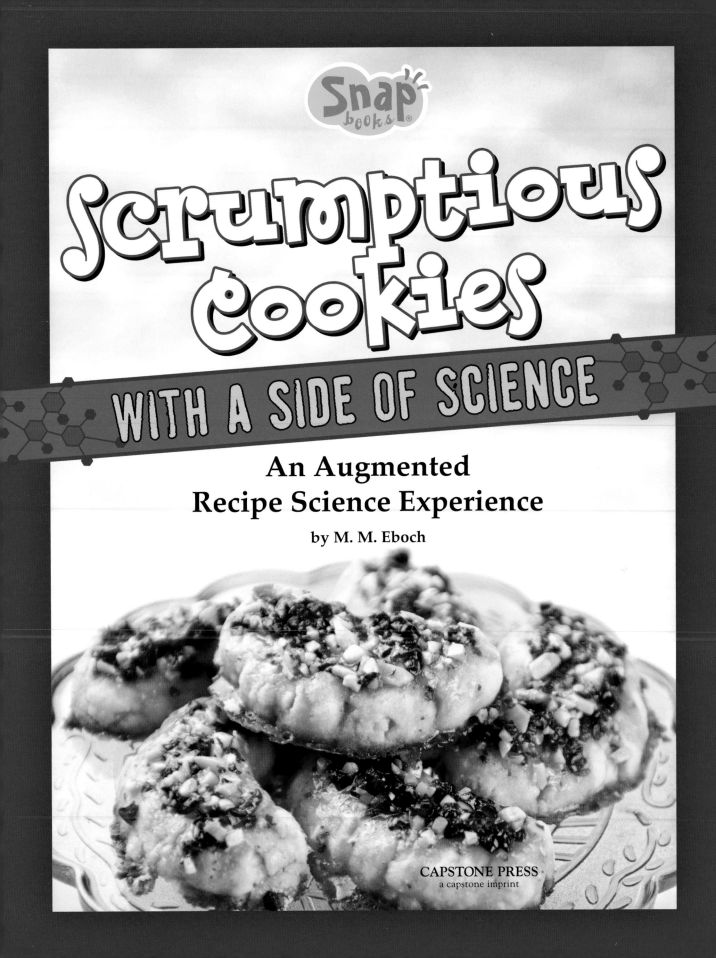

Scrumptious Cookies

WITH A SIDE OF SCIENCE

An Augmented
Recipe Science Experience

by M. M. Eboch

CAPSTONE PRESS
a capstone imprint

Download the Capstone 4D app!

- Ask an adult to download the Capstone 4D app.
- Scan the cover and stars inside the book for additional content.

When you scan a spread, you'll find fun extra stuff to go with this book! You can also find these things on the web at www.capstone4D.com using the password: cookies.10737

Snap Books are published by Capstone Press, 1710 Roe Crest Drive, North Mankato, Minnesota 56003
www.mycapstone.com

Library of Congress Cataloging-in-Publication Data
Names: Eboch, M. M., author.
Title: Scrumptious cookies with a side of science : 4D an augmented recipe science experience / by M. M. Eboch.
Description: North Mankato, Minnesota : Capstone Press, [2019] | Series: Snap books. Sweet eats with a side of science 4D | Audience: Age 9-14.
Identifiers: LCCN 2018012438 (print) | LCCN 2018014635 (eBook)
    ISBN 9781543510737 (library binding)
    ISBN 9781543510775 (eBook PDF)
Subjects: LCSH: Cookies—Juvenile literature. | LCGFT: Cookbooks.
Classification: LCC TX772 (eBook) | LCC TX772 .E28 2019 (print) | DDC 641.86/54—dc23
LC record available at https://lccn.loc.gov/2018012438

Editorial Credits
Abby Colich, editor; Juliette Peters, designer; Tracy Cummins, photo researcher; Laura Manthe, production specialist

Photo Credits
All images by Capstone Studio/Karon Dubke
Baker: Stephanie Lockling
Photo Stylist: Sarah Schuette

Printed in the United States of America.
PA017

Table of Contents

Let Your Baking Skills Rise 4

Apricot Shortbread 6

Flourless Peanut Butter Cookies 8

Flying Butterfly Cookies 10

Chocolate Covered Fortune Cookies 12

Two-For-One Cookie Dough Brownies 14

Chocolate Meringues with Raspberry Sauce 16

Cranberry Pistachio Biscotti 18

Almond Crescent Cookies with Fruity Garnish 20

Lemon-Frosted Sour Cream Cookies 22

Gingery Molasses Cookies 24

Microwave Oatmeal Cookie 26

Butterscotch Pecan Snow-Topped Mountains 28

Cookie Help 30

Glossary 31

Read More 32

Internet Sites 32

Cookies are great for beginning bakers. Toss some ingredients into a bowl, mix them well, drop on a cookie sheet, and bake. Soon you have a delicious dessert or satisfying snack.

What's that? You're not a beginning baker? Don't worry! Cookies are also great for developing your growing skills. Old favorites get an updated twist. Creative additions make basic recipes fancy. Frosting, glaze, and other toppings can make the cookies look as good as they taste.

The same is true for science in the kitchen. Whether you know a little or a lot, you can learn so much while baking. Science can help you understand what's happening in the oven. Why should you take cookies out of the oven before they are completely done baking? Why do most cookies bake at 350 degrees Fahrenheit? Why are some cookies crispy and others soft? The answers are more than fun facts. Knowing kitchen science will help you become an even better baker!

STAYING SAFE ★

Follow these tips to keep everyone safe in the kitchen:

- Wash your hands with soap and warm water before you start. Wash them often while you work, especially after handling raw eggs.

- Don't taste uncooked dough if it contains eggs. Raw eggs may make you sick.

- Ask an adult to help you use knives and other sharp objects.

- Use pot holders or oven mitts to handle hot items, such as baking sheets.

- Clean up any spills.

CONVERSION CHART

The recipes in this book use U.S. measurements. If you need metric measurements, here's a handy conversion guide.

VOLUME

1/4 teaspoon = 1.2 mL
1/2 teaspoon = 2.5 mL
1 teaspoon = 5 mL
1 tablespoon = 15 mL
1/4 cup = 60 mL
1/3 cup = 80 mL
1/2 cup = 120 mL
2/3 cup = 160 mL
3/4 cup = 180 mL
1 cup = 240 mL

WEIGHT

10 ounces = 280 grams
12 ounces = 340 grams

TEMPERATURE

200°F = 90°C
300°F = 150°C
350°F = 175°C
375°F = 190°C

TIP ....

Do you want more information about ingredients, mixing, or making cookies before you begin? Flip to page 30. Here you'll find a guide for some of the techniques used in this book.

Apricot Shortbread

Shortbread is wonderful by itself. It's buttery, flaky, and has just the right amount of sweetness. But you don't have to stop there. Add apricot preserves and a coconut macaroon layer. The result? A spectacular treat that will wow everyone who tries it!

INGREDIENTS
1 cup butter
1/2 cup sugar
2 teaspoons vanilla extract
1 teaspoon orange zest
2 cups all-purpose flour

TOPPING
12 ounces apricot preserves
1 large egg
1/2 cup sugar
1 teaspoon vanilla extract
2 tablespoons butter, melted
2 cups shredded coconut

SUPPLIES
baking sheet
electric mixer
mixing bowls
measuring cups and spoons
fork
spatula
sharp knife or pizza wheel

1 Preheat the oven to 350°F. Grease the baking sheet.

2 With electric mixer, blend the butter, sugar, vanilla extract, and orange zest. Mix in the flour until well combined.

3 Gather the dough into a ball. Press it into a flat circle on the baking sheet. It should be about 0.5 inch (1 cm) thick and about 9 inches (23 cm) across. Use a fork to prick the dough, covering the surface with little holes about 0.25 inch (0.5 cm) deep.

4 Spread apricot preserves on top of the dough.

5 To make the topping, beat the egg with a fork in a clean mixing bowl. Stir in the sugar, vanilla extract, butter, and coconut.

6 Drop spoonfuls of the coconut topping over the preserves. Spread evenly with a spatula.

7 Bake for 40 to 45 minutes, until lightly browned.

8 Let the shortbread rest on the baking sheet for 5 minutes.

9 Remove the shortbread from the pan and place it on a cutting board. Cut into 12 wedges using a sharp knife or a pizza wheel. Store in an airtight container.

TIP ....
Pricking small holes into the top allows steam to escape. The holes keep the shortbread from bubbling.

Kitchen Science
THE MAILLARD ⭐ REACTION

Special cooking reactions happen at different temperatures. At around 310 to 325°F (155 to 160°C), the Maillard reaction starts. It transforms sugars and amino acids, the building blocks of proteins. They recombine into hundreds of different mixtures. These new blends release smells and flavors. The Maillard reaction also causes browning. That's why most cookies turn golden as they bake. Most cookie recipes bake at 350°F (175°C). At much lower temperatures, the Maillard reaction won't happen. Your cookies might bake, but they won't brown, and they won't develop the complex flavors. At higher temperatures, cookies can cook too fast and burn.

Flourless Peanut Butter Cookies

A cookie without flour? It's almost unthinkable. Flour is one of the basic ingredients for cookies—most of the time! Even though this recipe doesn't use flour, it still has the flavor and texture of a peanut butter cookie. It's perfect for people who must avoid gluten, a protein in flour and other grains.

INGREDIENTS

1 cup peanut butter or
    sunflower seed butter
1 cup sugar
1 teaspoon baking soda
1 1/2 teaspoons salt
1 large egg
1 teaspoon vanilla extract
1/2 cup chopped peanuts

FROSTING

1/2 cup chocolate chips
2 tablespoons butter
1 1/4 cups confectioners' sugar
2 tablespoons milk

SUPPLIES

baking sheet
measuring cups and spoons
mixing bowls
electric mixer
fork
wire cooling rack

1 Preheat the oven to 350°F. Grease the baking sheet.

2 In a medium bowl, combine the peanut butter, sugar, baking soda, salt, egg, and vanilla extract. Mix until well blended.

3 Scoop up about 1 tablespoon of the mixture and roll it into a ball. Place on the cookie sheet. Repeat with remaining dough, placing balls at least 1 inch (2.5 cm) apart. Use a fork to flatten the balls.

4 Bake for 8 to 10 minutes, until golden around the edges. Let cookies rest on the pan for 5 minutes. Then transfer them to a rack to finish cooling.

5 To make the frosting, place chocolate chips and butter in a medium microwave-safe bowl. Microwave on high power for 30 seconds. Stir until smooth. If necessary, microwave an additional 10 seconds and stir. Repeat until chocolate is smooth with no lumps.

6 Add confectioners' sugar and milk. Stir until blended and smooth.

7 Spread frosting on each cookie. Sprinkle on chopped peanuts. Store cookies in an airtight container.

TIP....................................

You can make these with either creamy or crunchy peanut butter. All-natural peanut butter may add a gritty texture. Sunflower seed butter, also called sunbutter or sunflower spread, is made from sunflower seeds. It can be used like peanut butter for people allergic to peanuts.

Kitchen Science

HEAT TRANSFER ★

Cooking applies heat to foods to prepare them for eating. In scientific terms, heat is the transfer of energy from one object to another. Heat will transfer from a hotter substance to a cooler one. When baking, heat transfers from the warm air in the oven to the cookies and baking sheet. Once you remove them from the oven, they cool down. That's because heat transfers from the baking sheet and cookies to the cooler air. Eventually both the cookies and pan will reach room temperature—the same temperature as the air. They have reached thermal equilibrium. *Thermal* refers to heat. *Equilibrium* means an equal balance. Heat tends to transfer among objects until they are the same temperature.

Sugar cookies are simple, but there's nothing wrong with that when they taste so good! There are endless ways to shape and decorate sugar cookies. Try using a butterfly cookie cutter and decorating with colorful frosting. Insert a lollipop stick into each butterfly before it bakes, so it can "fly!"

INGREDIENTS

1 cup butter
1 cup sugar
1 egg
2 teaspoons vanilla extract
2 3/4 cups flour
1 teaspoon baking soda
1 teaspoon baking powder
1/2 teaspoon salt
extra flour for rolling out
    the cookies

FROSTING

3 cups confectioners' sugar
1/3 cup butter
2 teaspoons vanilla extract
1 to 2 tablespoons milk
food coloring

SUPPLIES

measuring cups and spoons
mixing bowls
electric mixer
cutting board
rolling pin
3-inch (7.5-cm) butterfly cookie cutters
baking sheets
lollipop sticks
wire cooling racks
pastry bags or zippered plastic bags

1 Place butter and sugar in a large mixing bowl. Cream with electric mixer until smooth. Beat in the egg and vanilla extract.

2 In a small bowl, stir together flour, baking soda, baking powder, and salt.

3 Blend the dry ingredients into the butter and sugar mixture. Refrigerate the dough for about 1 hour.

4 Preheat oven to 375°F. Sprinkle flour on a large, smooth cutting board. Place a fist-sized ball of dough in the middle. Use a rolling pin to roll the dough until it is 0.25 inch (0.5 cm) thick. Use cookie cutters to cut out butterfly shapes.

5 Place each cookie on an ungreased cookie sheet. Leave at least 1 inch (2.5 cm) between them. Leave enough room underneath each butterfly for the lollipop stick.

6 Gently insert one lollipop stick halfway into the center of each cookie.

7 Bake 9 to 12 minutes, until just barely starting to turn golden.

8 Let the cookies rest on the baking sheets for 5 minutes. Gently move them to wire racks to finish cooling.

9 To make the frosting, in a medium bowl blend the confectioners' sugar and butter. Blend in the vanilla extract and 1 tablespoon of milk. Add another tablespoon of milk if needed to make the frosting more spreadable.

10 Evenly divide the frosting into several small bowls. Add 2 to 3 drops of each color of food coloring to each bowl and blend well. Place each color of frosting in a separate pastry bag or plastic bag. If using plastic bags, seal each bag and snip off one lower corner.

11 Decorate the cookies once they are completely cool. Twist the top of the frosting bags to squeeze frosting out of the hole. Store in an airtight container.

TIP............................

You do not need to refrigerate the dough, but it becomes easier to handle if you do. With unrefrigerated dough, the cookies will bake faster, in 6 to 8 minutes.

Chocolate Covered Fortune Cookies

Would you take advice from a cookie? How about sending a message in a cookie? When you make fortune cookies, you can do exactly that. Write your own goofy fortunes, the sillier the better! Then make this treat even more special by dipping it in chocolate.

Your future will be filled with delicious cookies.

TIP.........................

Placing the fortune cookies in a muffin tin as they cool keeps the fold from opening back up.

INGREDIENTS

2 large egg whites
1/2 teaspoon vanilla extract
1/2 teaspoon almond extract
3 tablespoons vegetable oil
1/2 cup all-purpose flour
1/2 cup sugar
1/4 teaspoon salt
1 tablespoon water

2/3 cup dark chocolate chips
2/3 cup white chocolate chips

SUPPLIES

paper and pen
scissors
baking sheets
nonstick cooking spray
measuring cups and spoons
mixing bowls and spoon
spatula
muffin tin

1 Cut a piece of paper into about 10 small strips, each about 3 x 0.25 inches (7.5 x 0.5 cm). Write fortunes or messages on them.

2 Preheat oven to 300°F. Spray baking sheets with nonstick cooking spray.

3 Place the egg whites, vanilla and almond extracts, and vegetable oil into a medium bowl. Beat until frothy.

4 In another bowl, blend the flour, sugar, and salt. Blend in the water.

5 Combine the two mixtures. Stir until you have a smooth batter.

6 Place a level tablespoon of batter onto the baking sheet. Use the back of a spoon to spread it into a 2-inch (5-cm) circle. Repeat, spacing the cookies at least 3 inches (7.5 cm) apart. (The batter spreads as it bakes, so no more than two cookies will fit on a baking sheet. Save the rest of the batter for later. Cookies must be folded and formed quickly, so it's best not to do them all at once.)

7 Bake 10 to 12 minutes, until the outer edge of each cookie is golden brown. Using a spatula, flip each cookie onto a clean work surface. Quickly place a fortune in the middle of each cookie. Fold the cookies in half, then gently bend the edges downward. Use caution as the cookies will be hot. Place each finished cookie in the cup of a muffin tin.

8 Repeat steps 6 and 7 until you've used all the batter. Let the cookies cool.

9 Place the dark chocolate chips in a small, microwave-safe bowl. Microwave on high power for 30 seconds. Stir until smooth. If necessary, microwave at additional 10-second intervals. After each interval, stir until smooth.

10 Dip one half of each fortune cookie into the dark chocolate.

11 Repeat step 9 with the white chocolate. Drizzle each fortune cookie with the melted white chocolate. Return them to the baking sheet and chill in the refrigerator until the chocolate is firm. Store in an airtight container.

Kitchen Science

RESIDUAL COOKING ★

When you take a hot dish out of the oven, it takes time to cool. As long as the food is still hot, it keeps cooking. This is called residual cooking or carryover cooking. It affects many cooked foods, including baked cookies. In order to bake cookies perfectly, you should take them out of the oven before they look done. Leave them on the cookie sheet for 3 to 5 minutes. (This is sometimes called "resting" a food.) The heat from the cookie sheet will continue to bake the cookies. Then move the cookies to a wire rack to finish cooling. The wire rack lets air flow all around each cookie so it cools quickly and evenly.

Two-For-One Cookie Dough Brownies

Dense, chewy chocolate brownies are so good, but chocolate chip cookies are amazing too. How do you choose which to make? With this recipe, you don't need to! A rich brownie layer is topped with raw chocolate chip cookie dough. The cookie dough layer does not contain eggs, so it's safe to eat.

INGREDIENTS	COOKIE DOUGH LAYER	SUPPLIES

4 large eggs
1 1/4 cups unsweetened cocoa
   powder
1 teaspoon salt
1 teaspoon baking powder
1 tablespoon vanilla extract
1 cup butter
2 1/4 cups sugar
1 1/2 cups flour
	1/2 cup butter
	1/4 cup sugar
	1/2 cup packed brown sugar
	3 tablespoons milk
	1 teaspoon vanilla extract
	1 cup flour
	1 cup chocolate chips
		baking pan, 9 x 13 inches
		   (23 x 33 cm)
		mixing bowls
		measuring cups and spoons
		electric mixer
		wire cooling rack

1 Preheat oven to 350°F. Grease the baking pan.

2 In a mixing bowl, lightly beat the eggs. Add the cocoa, salt, baking powder, and vanilla extract. Beat at medium speed for about 1 minute, until smooth.

3 In a medium microwave-safe bowl, melt the butter. Add the sugar and stir to combine.

4 Add the butter and sugar mixture to the other ingredients and stir to combine. Blend in the flour.

5 Pour the batter into the baking pan. Bake for 28 to 32 minutes. Use a cake tester or toothpick inserted into the center to test doneness. It should come out clean or with only a few moist crumbs clinging to it. Place the pan on a cooling rack.

6 Make the cookie dough layer. Cream the butter and both sugars in a mixing bowl. Blend in the milk and vanilla extract. Blend in the flour. Stir in the chocolate chips.

7 Drop spoonfuls of cookie dough over the cooled brownies. Spread the cookie dough layer evenly. Cut the brownies into squares or bars and store them in the refrigerator in an airtight container.

Kitchen Science
SWEET AND SOFT ★

White sugar and brown sugar are similar. They both come from sugar cane or sugar beets. Yet the two sugars act quite differently in baked goods. All sugar is hygroscopic, meaning it absorbs moisture from the air. Brown sugar is more hygroscopic than white sugar. Brown sugar naturally contains 10 times as much moisture as white sugar. This extra moisture means cookies made with brown sugar are softer. Dark brown sugar has more moisture than light brown sugar. Therefore, using dark brown sugar will result in the softest cookies. Using only white sugar will yield crisper cookies. In humid climates, the air holds a lot of moisture. Cookies become softer over time, as they absorb moisture from the air.

Chocolate Meringues with Raspberry Sauce

Egg whites and sugar may not sound very exciting. But mix them well and bake them slowly, and you get meringues. These delicate sweets are as light as clouds!

INGREDIENTS

3 egg whites, at room temperature
1/4 teaspoon cream of tartar
3/4 cup confectioners' sugar
1 teaspoon vanilla extract
4 tablespoons unsweetened cocoa powder, sifted

RASPBERRY SAUCE

10 ounces fresh or frozen raspberries
1/2 cup confectioners' sugar
2 teaspoons lemon juice

SUPPLIES

baking sheets
parchment paper
pastry bag with large star tip
mixing bowls
electric mixer
measuring cups and spoons
spatula
blender

1 Preheat oven to 200°F. Spread parchment paper on the baking sheets. Prepare the pastry bag with a large star tip.

2 In a large bowl, beat the egg whites with an electric mixer until frothy.

3 In a separate bowl, blend the cream of tartar and confectioners' sugar. Add this mixture to the egg whites, 1 tablespoon at a time, mixing between each addition.

4 Beat until the egg whites are stiff and shiny. Add the vanilla extract and cocoa. Reduce speed to low and mix to combine.

5 Use a spatula to scoop the egg white mixture into the pastry bag. Squeeze out a round disk of meringue, about 2 inches (5 cm) across, on a baking sheet. Pipe another layer of meringue in a circle around the edge, so you have a small bowl. Repeat with the remaining batter, leaving at least 2 inches (5 cm) between each meringue.

6 Bake for 2 hours. Turn off oven but leave the meringues inside for at least 2 more hours. The meringues are ready when they are completely dry.

7 Make the dipping sauce. Put the raspberries, confectioners' sugar, and lemon juice in a blender. Puree until smooth and combined. (If using frozen raspberries, thaw them first and let any extra liquid drain off.)

8 Store meringues in an airtight container. Use parchment paper to separate each layer of cookies. Store the sauce separately. When you are ready to serve the meringues, spoon a bit of raspberry sauce into the center or drizzle on top of each.

TIP..............................

Because sugar is hygroscopic, it attracts and holds water molecules from the air. Because meringues are mostly sugar, they can get soggy easily. Avoid making meringues on humid days. Moisture in the air makes it difficult for the meringues to dry properly. And add raspberries only to the meringues you expect to eat right away.

Cranberry Pistachio Biscotti

How about a cookie that is simply made for dipping? Crispy biscotti are often dipped in a hot drink to soften them. Try them dunked in hot cocoa. Biscotti get their firm, crispy texture from being baked twice. In Italian *biscotti* means "twice baked."

INGREDIENTS

2 cups flour, plus more if needed
2 teaspoons baking powder
1/4 teaspoon salt
1 teaspoon orange zest
1 cup sugar
1/4 cup cornstarch
3/4 cup orange juice

2 tablespoons coconut oil
1 teaspoons vanilla or
  almond extract
1 cup dried cranberries
1 cup whole, shelled pistachios
2 tablespoons sugar to
  sprinkle on top

SUPPLIES

baking sheet
measuring cups and spoons
mixing bowls
electric mixer
wire cooling rack
serrated knife
cutting board

1 Preheat oven to 350°F. Grease the baking sheet.

2 In a medium bowl, stir together the flour, baking powder, salt, and orange zest. Set aside.

3 In a large bowl, stir together the sugar and cornstarch. Add the orange juice and blend with an electric mixer for about 3 minutes. Add the coconut oil and extract. Beat for another 3 minutes.

4 Add the flour mixture to the sugar mixture and blend. Stir in the cranberries and pistachios.

5 Form the dough into a ball. If the dough is too sticky, add flour a tablespoon at a time. Add up to 4 tablespoons, until you can form a firm ball.

6 Divide the dough in half. Form each half into a log about 12 x 3 inches (30.5 x 7.5 cm). Place the logs on the baking sheet.

7 Sprinkle 1 tablespoon of sugar on top of each log.

8 Bake for 30 minutes. Cool on a wire rack for 15 minutes.

9 Place a log on a cutting board. Use a serrated knife to slice the log into 1-inch (2.5-cm) slices. Return these slices to the baking sheet. Bake 7 to 10 minutes. Flip slices and bake another 7 to 10 minutes. Repeat with the other log. Cool the slices on a wire rack. Store biscotti in an airtight container.

TIP...

Using coconut oil instead of butter makes this recipe dairy free and vegan.

Almond Crescent Cookies with Fruity Garnish

These cookies look like little crescent moons, and they taste heavenly. Almond crescents, or *Vanillekipferl*, originated in Austria. The recipe is simple except for one tricky step. The cookie dough is a bit crumbly. It might take you a couple tries to form the crescents without breaking the cookies! But don't worry if you have a few cracks. The fruit topping cleverly hides any mistakes.

INGREDIENTS	FRUIT TOPPING	SUPPLIES
1 cup butter	1/3 cup mixed berries or candied fruit	baking sheets
2/3 cup sugar	1/3 cup slivered almonds	nonstick cooking spray
1 teaspoon vanilla extract	1/4 cup butter	measuring cups and spoons
1 teaspoon almond extract	1/4 cup honey	mixing bowls
2 1/2 cups flour	1/4 cup apricot jam	electric mixer
1 cup almond flour		wire cooling rack
		small saucepan
		miniature cookie cutters

1 Preheat oven to 350°F. Spray the baking sheets with nonstick cooking spray.

2 Cream the butter and the sugar together until light and fluffy. Blend in the vanilla and almond extracts.

3 Add the flour and almond flour and mix well. The dough will be slightly crumbly.

4 Take a spoonful of dough and roll it into a 1-inch (2.5-cm) ball. Shape the ball into a crescent. Place it onto a baking sheet. Repeat with the remaining dough, placing the crescents at least 2 inches (5 cm) apart.

5 To make the fruit topping, finely chop the berries or candied fruit. Combine in blender with the slivered almonds, butter, and honey. Spread the mixture on the crescents.

6 Bake for 12 to 15 minutes. Let them rest on the baking sheets for 5 minutes, then transfer to a rack to cool.

7 Heat apricot jam in a small saucepan over medium heat until syrupy. Drizzle jam over the tops of each cookie. Store cookies in an airtight container.

TIP......................................

Almond flour may also be called almond meal. Look for it among the gluten-free products of a grocery store or in health food stores.

Kitchen Science

ADDING AIR ⭐

When baking cookies, you need to mix the ingredients in order to blend them together. In this recipe you *cream* the butter and sugar. Creaming is a form of mixing, but it doesn't merely blend the ingredients. It also *aerates* them, or adds air. You are folding the dough over and over, adding little pockets of air. Creaming butter and sugar together mixes fat (from the butter), sugar crystals, and air. In the oven that air expands as it heats. The pockets of air help the cookies rise. If you like a flatter, denser cookie, don't cream the butter and sugar. Simply mix them together enough to blend the ingredients.

Lemon-Frosted Sour Cream Cookies

If you like cake, you'll love these sour cream cookies. They are soft and tender with a cakey texture that melts in your mouth. A vivid lemon flavor balances out this delicate cookie. Lemon frosting adds even more citrus zing, while edible glitter gives it a sparkle.

INGREDIENTS

1/4 cup butter
1 cup sugar
2 large eggs
1/3 cup sour cream
1 tablespoon lemon zest
    (from 2 lemons)
1 tablespoon lemon juice
    (from 1 lemon)
2 cups all-purpose flour
1/4 teaspoon baking soda
2 teaspoons baking powder

FROSTING

1/4 cup butter
1 1/2 cups confectioners' sugar
1 tablespoon lemon juice
    (from 1 lemon)
2 to 3 drops yellow food
    coloring, optional
edible glitter or candy
    sprinkles

SUPPLIES

baking sheets
parchment paper
mixing bowls
measuring cups and spoons
electric mixer
wire cooling rack
butter knife

1 Preheat the oven to 350°F. Line the baking sheets with parchment paper.

2 Place the butter and sugar in a large bowl. Beat with the electric mixer until smooth, about 3 minutes.

3 Add the eggs, sour cream, lemon zest, and lemon juice. Mix until well blended.

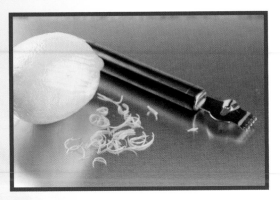

4 In a separate bowl, blend the flour, baking soda, and baking powder. Add to the butter mixture and stir until just combined. The dough will be sticky and soft, like a thick cake batter.

5 Drop the dough by heaping spoonfuls onto the baking sheets, at least 2 inches (5 cm) apart. Bake for 10 to 12 minutes, until the centers are firm and the edges are golden.

6 Let cookies rest on the pan for 5 minutes, then transfer to a rack to cool.

7 Make the frosting. Beat the butter and sugar until smooth. Add 1 tablespoon lemon juice and the food coloring and blend well. If needed, add a little water to make a spreadable, smooth, and thick frosting.

8 Frost the cookies when they are completely cooled. Swirl the frosting onto the cookies with a butter knife. Sprinkle with edible glitter or candy sprinkles. Store cookies in an airtight container.

Gingery Molasses Cookies

Fragrant spices and molasses make this a perfect cookie to warm you up on a chilly day. Chewy candied ginger adds even more heat and flavor. The cookie batter is very soft at first because of the liquid molasses. Chilling it in the fridge turns the runny batter into a firm dough. The dough needs to be chilled for several hours, so plan accordingly.

INGREDIENTS

3/4 cup butter
1 cup sugar
1/4 cup molasses
1 egg
2 cups flour
1/2 teaspoon salt
2 teaspoons baking soda
1 teaspoon cinnamon
1 teaspoon ginger
1/2 teaspoon cloves
1/2 cup chopped crystallized ginger

ICING

1 cup confectioners' sugar
1 to 2 tablespoons real maple syrup

SUPPLIES

electric mixer
mixing bowls
measuring cups and spoons
plastic wrap
muffin tin
nonstick cooking spray
wire cooling rack
spoon for drizzling

1 In a large bowl, mix the butter, sugar, molasses, and egg.

2 In a separate bowl, stir together the flour, salt, baking soda, and all spices. Pour this into the butter mixture and blend well. Stir in the crystallized ginger.

3 Cover the bowl with plastic wrap and chill in refrigerator for several hours or overnight.

4 Preheat oven to 350°F. Spray the cups of a muffin tin with nonstick cooking spray. Scoop spoonfuls of dough and roll them into 2-inch (5-cm) balls in your hands. Place each ball in the cup of a muffin tin.

5 For soft, gooey cookies, bake about 10 minutes, until the edges look firm but the middle is still very soft. If you like crisper cookies, bake 12 to 14 minutes, until they look firm in the middle.

6 Rest the cookies in the muffin tin for 5 minutes. Then remove the cookies and set on a wire rack to finish cooling.

7 Make the icing. In small bowl, blend confectioners' sugar and 1 tablespoon maple syrup. Add more maple syrup if needed for consistency. The icing should be thin enough to drizzle from a spoon. Drizzle the icing over the cookies in a zigzag pattern. Store in an airtight container.

TIP ·

Dark molasses gives the cookies a stronger molasses flavor. Light or mild molasses adds less of the flavor.

Microwave Oatmeal Cookie

Baking cookies can be a lot of fun, but sometimes you want a treat now. These cookies take only 5 minutes to make! They are perfect for when you want a sweet treat but don't have a lot of time. Microwave cookies are best eaten right away. Otherwise they can quickly get hard or soggy. This recipe makes a single serving. No waiting and no leftovers!

INGREDIENTS

1/4 cup quick-cooking oats
2 teaspoons flour
2 teaspoons brown sugar
1/4 teaspoon baking powder
dash of cinnamon
2 tablespoons applesauce

1/4 teaspoon vanilla extract
1 tablespoon raisins

SUPPLIES

mixing bowl
microwave-safe plate
measuring cups and spoons
nonstick cooking spray

1 In a small bowl, mix the oats, flour, brown sugar, baking powder, and cinnamon.

2 Stir in the applesauce and vanilla extract and mix. Stir in the raisins.

3 Spray a microwave-safe plate with cooking spray. Scoop the dough onto the plate. Press it into a cookie shape.

4 Microwave cookie on high for 60 seconds. Let sit in microwave for 1 minute. If cookie still looks doughy, reheat for an additional 10 seconds. Repeat if needed.

TIP....................

Cooking times can vary among microwaves. You may need to experiment to find the right cooking time for this recipe.

Kitchen Science

MICROWAVE COOKING

A microwave oven uses electromagnetic radiation. These are waves of electrical and magnetic energy that move through space. In other words, a microwave creates energy waves. These waves penetrate the food. They cause water molecules in the food to vibrate. The friction caused by the vibrating heats the food. Many foods cook more quickly in a microwave than in a regular oven. However, the air in a microwave is not heated. That means microwaves can't brown the surface of most foods. Because browning is important in most baking, ovens are usually more ideal.

Butterscotch Pecan Snow-Topped Mountains

You don't have to climb mountains to make these cookies. In fact, you don't even have to bake them! It's easy to change up this recipe. Instead of the pretzel sticks, try oats, granola, crispy rice cereal, or even crispy chow mein noodles. Try different nuts, raisins, or chocolate chips. Make this recipe your own!

INGREDIENTS

2 cups butterscotch chips
1/2 cup pecans, chopped
1 cup miniature pretzel sticks, each
   broken in half
1 cup milk chocolate chips
1/2 cup sweetened shredded coconut

SUPPLIES

baking sheet
parchment paper
measuring cups
microwave-safe bowls

1 Line a baking sheet with parchment paper.

2 Place the butterscotch chips in a microwave-safe bowl. Microwave for 1 minute. Stir to blend. Microwave for 15 seconds more if needed to melt the chips. Stir until smooth.

3 Add the chopped pecans and broken pretzel sticks and mix well.

4 Drop the cookie mixture by heaping spoonfuls onto the paper. Quickly press them into cone "mountain" shapes. Refrigerate the cookies until they are firm, about 1 hour.

5 Place the milk chocolate chips in a microwave-safe bowl. Microwave for 30 seconds and stir until smooth. If necessary, microwave for additional 10-second intervals.

6 Dip the top two-thirds of each cookie into the milk chocolate. Place the cookie back on the baking sheet and sprinkle with shredded coconut. Refrigerate until the chocolate hardens, at least 30 minutes.

7 Store the cookies in an airtight container in the refrigerator. Set out at room temperature for 10 minutes before eating.

Cookie Help

Get great cookies every time by following some basic steps.

BAKING TIPS

• Use unsalted butter unless the recipe says otherwise. Butter and eggs should be at room temperature. Take them out of the refrigerator at least 30 minutes before you start baking.

• Put an oven rack on the middle shelf of the oven. Then turn on your oven and let it fully preheat, at least 15 minutes. These steps help ensure the cookies bake evenly.

• Most recipes assume the baker is close to sea level. If you live 3,500 feet (1,050 meters) or more above sea level, you may need to adjust your oven temperature. Many online resources provide instructions.

• To grease a baking sheet, rub a very thin layer of butter on the pan with a paper towel.

• Flour that is packed down into the measuring cup will be way more than you need. Use a spoon to scoop flour into your measuring cup. Sprinkle it in lightly and do not tap it down. Use the back of a knife to level off the top.

• Measure all other ingredients carefully. Use full cups or spoons with the ingredient level across the top, not piled up. Brown sugar is the only ingredient you need to pack down into the cup.

• To get orange or lemon zest, use a fine grater. Shave slivers of the darkest outside part of the peel.

• Set a timer for the lowest time mentioned in the recipe. When the timer dings, check the cookies. Remove them when they look almost, but not quite, finished.

PROPER MIXING

You may see several mixing terms, with slight differences in meaning:

• **blend**—to mix ingredients until they are well combined and smooth

• **beat**—to mix ingredients well and add in air, either with a mixer or with a spoon, using an up-and-down and circular motion; beating until something is frothy means it is foamy and has tiny air bubbles

• **cream**—to mix sugar and a fat such as butter until smooth, light, and creamy

• **whip**—to make a mixture light and fluffy by beating vigorously

• When mixing, use a spatula to scrape dough from the bottom and sides of the bowl to the center. This helps combine ingredients well.

Glossary

aerate—to introduce air into a material

amino acid—a building block of protein made by cells in the body from substances obtained by food in the diet

energy—the ability to do work; energy exists in several forms, including heat

equilibrium—a state in which opposing forces are balanced

gluten—a protein found in some grains and flours that helps hold dough together and makes it sticky

heat—the transfer of energy from one object to another

heat transfer—the process by which heat moves from one substance to another

hygroscopic—easily absorbing moisture from the air

Maillard reaction—the reaction between amino acids and sugar that browns foods and causes a distinctive flavor

protein—a substance that is essential for growth and to repair damage to the body

residual—remaining after the greater part has gone

temperature—the degree of hotness or coldness of something

thermal—relating to heat

Read More

Besel, Jen. *Custom Confections: Delicious Desserts You Can Create and Enjoy.* North Mankato, Minn.: Capstone Young Readers, 2015.

The Exploratorium. *Exploring Kitchen Science: 30+ Edible Experiments and Kitchen Science Activities.* San Francisco: Weldon Owen, 2015.

Schloss, Andrew. *Amazing (Mostly) Edible Science: A Family Guide to Fun Experiments in the Kitchen.* Beverly, Mass.: Quarry, 2016.

Internet Sites

Use FactHound to find Internet sites related to this book.

Visit *www.facthound.com*

Just type in 9781543510737 and go.

 Check out projects, games and lots more at
www.capstonekids.com